AN EROTIC COLLECTION

FREYA RAY

The Taste of Skin copyright © 2026 by Freya Ray.

All rights reserved. No part of this publication may be reproduced, distributed, or transmitted in any form by any means, including photocopying, recoarding, or other electronic methods without the prior written permission of the author, except in the case of brief quotations embodied in reviews and certain other noncommercial uses permitted by copyright law. For permission requests, write to the author at the address below.

Freya Ray
Freyaanneray@gmail.com

www.freyaannerayy.com

CONTENT WARNING: this collection contains descriptive scenes of nudity.

Illustrations: Johanna Barbara
Formatting and Design: Freya Ray

ISBN: 979-8-9866993-1-8

Printed in the United States of America.

the taste of skin

AN EROTIC COLLECTION

FREYA RAY

content

YOU   11

HIM   71

THEY   117

foreword

this is a collection of poems that poured through me during a time in my life where i was becoming. it was the first season i had reclaimed my skin as my own, and intimacy in these times was something i had never known before. each movement, each breath, each partner was a yes, a choice of my own. the first time poetry found me it was when i was dancing with darkness, heavy skin and bones and love to me was not intimate. but in the wake of my body being taken, i vowed to come back home to her and it is through these poems my path formed. this is not all of what love means to me, but for a woman who was taught that love would never become better, that explorations were limited to the body rather than the soul, these pages are a reclamation. and the gift each of the lovers i had as these poems formed has been the most beautiful magic to witness. we truly are love, and in connection that knowing shines like nothing else. love is beautiful, sex is magical, intimacy is gorgeous, and heartbreak is a gift. so if you are one of my lovers, thank you. and if you are a witness to the magic that can be born when you lay down the bias that has been taught about what and how love is meant to form then i hope these poems honour the love that has been. these poems are written about he's, she's, and they's, all are welcome here and i do hope one of the poems may resonate for you in an experience of your own.
many of these poems are explicit, be discerning as you read.

YOU.

the way my lips express themselves
at the thought of you,
a honeysuckle unveiled for the sun.

THE TASTE OF SKIN

my mind lost between the realms
of this one and heaven-
presently awake. my heart beats-
tapped into a timeline
where our skin vibrates
against one another.
surely i'm just building upon the memory
of that first time you felt me.

the way your lips softened against mine-
so kind, so out of line i was, and yet
so vulgarly affectionate we were
for having met only five hours before.
tequila coursing through my veins,
your tongue exploring mine,
nowhere near enough could be given
before i awoke-
realized.
the way time had dissolved
the moment you kissed me,
with your hand gentle against my cheek.
i must go echoed through heavy breath
until i crawled inside my bed and imagined
your taste in my mouth-
the beast inside reignited
her tamed time in life-
a revolution, the awakening
of my own divine right-
my body melting into ritual,
calling your name.

your name.
i know no more than **your name.**

these dreams i've been having
are reactivating the parts of me
that remember how to fall
so intimately **into you.**

admit it—
>   *i'm in love with you.*
the way your breasts breathe
against your skin.
the way your heart opens
for far too many to come in.
your body, the way she radiates
full resonance.

maybe i can just feel you,
with empathy too deep
for even my own understanding.

or maybe **i am in love with you**—
my hands unconsciously cloud my eyes
in fabrics of silk, soft to the touch,
and yet just thick enough
to hide my projection of lust.

i notice the way they look at you,
the way they lust for your attention,
beg for your desire to beseech you—
a moment of melancholy
to rise within you.
no matter.
numbers of men—timid cognizance
of them alive within me.
yet amongst them, i am breathing,
understanding their lust,
their love,
this allure you have
from which they cannot break free.

still, i withstand
this tunnel vision
you have for your man—
for his arm around you
turns their heads as you walk by,
but not mine.
how lucky i am.
i cry.

i wonder sometimes if you notice—
the way i see you,
appreciate you,
the way i wish you could imagine
what it means to fall for a woman
who will never see you
as **more than a friend.**

is it possible that it has **always** been you?

you are not what i thought you'd be.
a whole lifetime of knowing you, and
never did i dream of the way you would
hold your body on top of me—
the way you'd feel soft, or sturdy,
or gently touch every inch of me.
never did i dream of the way you would kiss,
or the softness of your lips against
my thighs, my hips.
never did i dream that your energy would be so heavenly,
confident, and so respectful you'd be.
never did i dream that you would know exactly how
how to activate erotic intimacy,
dance within the flames god created inside humanity.
never did i dream that your heart would speak so loudly,
that your presence would arouse me,
birth my body back into tantric sensuality.
never did i dream that you would reference me
to be sweet like honey,
and yet as you felt me,
all i could think was,
honey, that's you.

THE TASTE OF SKIN

i want you to be **soaking wet**
dripping against my skin,
my fingers,
my lips,
a flood between your legs
before you welcome me in.

empty promises look a whole lot like **charisma**tic words
when they come from you.

when **i ache for you** to whisper against my skin
the things you would do to me,
to speak in monologue
with fire in your breath,
i am waiting for your letter in reply.
my heart fond of silence,
and still your resonance anticipated.

such **valor** you hold in the face of sensuality,
this love is heaven and you are divinity.

THE TASTE OF SKIN

i rarely get stumped,
but you walked in like the wind.
i was so overtaken by the heaviness
that as my jaw turned toward you,

>i was already off my feet
>stumbling across the street
>wondering what just happened.

i rarely indulge in desire,
but i find myself looking at you
with wide eyes—
the kind that pull apart
the fabric of the universe—
because i can see through anyone
but i cant seem to see through you.
i rarely escape my lack of trust,
but with you, it feels easy.
my body softens at your touch and—
i rarely grasp onto touch
because the times it felt like rust
were endless. i feel
subtle shifts in my consciousness.
you've evaporated every sense
of necessary love,
and it's become timeless.
i rarely fall in love,
but the stories they told—
how you'd just fall for fun—
made me feel invincible.
like i could stay so in control
that my heart wouldn't run
through the pages.
i rarely find someone untouched.
i've listened to your walk through life,
and each time we found a new dusk before dawn—
one where we're silent—
i tend to pause, expansively,
existing in the **rarities**
of just us.

you have a gentleness to you,
the way you shift from sweet to strengthened
present and yet activation lie
dormant within your eyes-
god really handcrafted even your **insides**.

hearts don't belong on sleeves-
my mind would say.

       i love you-
       are you real?
my heart was fluttering away.

      why can't i read you?
      sounds unhealthy;
     maybe i shouldn't stay-
the thought patterns of a woman
who just escaped an abusive space.

         is this it?-
constantly in wonder if i actually surpassed
not wanting more than just this.

      you make me happy;
       i want this-
my heart jumps forward across time,
so fast my mind is quick to
configure the broken mends.

   he can't also be feeling this-
these voices in my head feel endless.

      do i deserve this?-
my body shuttered off timid thoughts,
for she opened like a flower at the
energy he brought.

   maybe the point in this is just
      to remember
      what love is-

my heart's pulse stood at a stop.

the timid taste
of your soft and salty skin
against my tongue
reminds me of my lips
after the ocean has kissed my lungs.

THE TASTE OF SKIN

oh sweet **nectar**, i had no clue
you were so close within grasp,
within this man, i have found you.
and i will savor every taste
as i kiss your lips, every crevice—
i want all of you.
i want you to taste all of me,
as if i'm that sweet pastry
you melt into in the morning.
i want you to feel me
as i fall so lucidly into your body,
into your mind, allow me to caress
my tongue against the most divine parts of you.

i want your hands to glide across my skin,
tease my mind as you grasp all the curvatures
that were made for your handling—
my hips
my lips
my neck
my breasts
my stomach
my back
my thighs
wrap my ankles around you
as i merge into you.

tell me you love me—
let me moan it back to you.
feel yourself inside me,
our energies dancing in the inbetween.

oh sweet nectar,
the way you kiss me
as if you're the heavens.
as i breathe in earth,
you're softly telling me
you're with me.

today i thought about the way you licked
the roof of my mouth,
the way your skin felt on mine
when the darkness left no sounds,
the way your hands slid around my back—
grabbed my waist, and settled down,
the way you melted into my energy,
the rhythm we so innocently found.

today i thought about the sweetness
of your lips, the calming nature of your hands
when they held the back of my neck.
i thought about the feeling of my hips
wrapped around yours:
this timeless puzzle made from heaven.

i thought about that time i bit your lip,
the way your body sweetened.
i thought about the way you sound,
the rawness of your voice
when no one else is around.

i thought about the honesty of you,
the gift of presence you carry—reflective hues.

i thought about the remedy of your skin,
but more of your laughter, the tilt of your lips.

i thought about your hands,
their imprint upon my skin.
i thought about moving your
wrist
upward across my body
to land **your handprint** across my chest.

i thought about the way you'd react
when we finally decided to exist
solely within one another's depth.

i still hear your voice in my head-
the way i'd breathe the words
and you'd play the melody.
it was heaven.

you were **heavenly.**

and one day,
you will be relished too.
you will be sucked, licked, twisted,
k
   i
      s
         s
            e
               d ,

                                      flipped,
and honoured in every second.
you, my dear, will be worshipped.
may you howl to the moon while they
p   l   e   a   s   u   r   e   you,
and may the sun blanket your skin
like your own **erotic tapestry**
after hours of intimacy.

call me **foreign** and
i will explore the insides of your mind
while your body rests in the deep.
the ember of your eye will ache
as your vision remembers how perfectly
our bodies became melodies.
i'll carve into your soul the sigil
we once burned into the sky as we felt
                                    anything but foreign.

the love i am going to make with you
will be something this world has never **felt** before.

this morning i awoke
to your voice in my head
the sweet silhouette
of your vocals untamed
you drew me back from
once again **mending**
the realms between
time and space.

and what if i fall in love with you?
the same thoughts as the girl before me
rush through my mind.
what if the way you smile echoes within me
for days or weeks or months after our tides collapse?
or the way you laugh reminds me of the way he laughed-
the last one i loved so deeply that left so suddenly?
what if the separation of our skin
feels like cutting bondage from my hips
in a moment of suffocation-
unexpected and yet so intimately eloquent?
what if i fall in love with the concept
of falling in love with you?
and for these days ahead of me,
i remember what it feels like
to breathe in ecstasy.
what if i fall in love with falling again?
what **an unkept gift** the gods may have handed to me.

the dichotomy of this perception of you
is exhilarating **my bones** into this realm
where anything is possible.
is it possible?
are we?

all of u is *permanently burned* into my memory

                                                              2:15 pm

my body is **aching** for your skin,
your coarse and yet soft fingers
moving between my lips,
the way your hands wrap so perfectly
around my hips.

my body aches for you again,
my dreams filled with lustful moments
of love made between tongues,
a melody playing against our souls
as we exist within one another.

my body aches to feel whole,
for that union residing in legends,
the moment written in the stars—
two flames burning into one.

my body aches for your touch,
but even more so, my soul aches
for your love.

THE TASTE OF SKIN

electric kisses against my skin,
your body elastic at my fingertips,
dewdrops dripping down my thighs.

make love to me whispers my third eye,
both my conscious and unconscious mind
tapping into your light.

show me your
d
i
v
i
n
e.

i want you
in ways i never want anyone.
i want you to slide inside of me—
frequencies of love that explode fountains
from parts of my being i never thought could erupt.
i want you to love me, like you've never loved anyone,
and i don't want just anyone to love me—
i want you.

you're kind of like candy-
sweet to the tongue,
your words wrapped in delicacy,
chocolate + caramel bursts underneath.
the depth of your soul
is what makes you so rich;
the softness of your heart
any woman's dream-an endless breath.
and yet the wondering of your eyes
when our moments disconnect
make me wonder if this candy
is a handmade chocolate
you cannot dream ever did exist.
or, if your wrappers are made
of a falsified tin
and your candy processed
like a ferrero rocher's is.
either way, whether this tease is true
or if its cotton truth,
i wonder if your heart is
as real as you.
and still,
i find that my heart is whispering to my mind:
will the rush will end as candies tend to?

THE TASTE OF SKIN

the satin of your words
as they grace my tongue
laying **salt** upon my tastebuds
feels like my blood against your lungs-
foreign and meant to be
all at once

tattoo-wrapped skin lays against mine,
deep caramel gliding against my hips
hands so kind, holding my neck,
soft kisses against my breath.

THE TASTE OF SKIN

open roads before my eyes,
my gaze locks in the space
between visuals and time.
memory gifts me a moment of you and i—
your hands inside liquifying tides,
my mouth **unruly** between your hips and thighs.
heat climbs upward through my body,
waves of desire igniting my insides,
ecstatic pleasures salivating my tongue,
milky textures falling from our skin
like hot caramel from an apple's edge.
the only thought in my head,
o v e r
and
over
a
  g
    a
      i
        n:
i can't get enough of this,
of you.

thin white chocolate dribbles down my thighs,
warm like **caramel** drizzled upon apple pies.
your tongue grazes my stomach line,
each inch of my skin just salty enough
that my body was made
to be tasted
by your tongue.

saliva glides towards the back of my hips
as your fingers slip inside me and
as your tongue is slick against my clit.

i love the way your tattoos look
when the light touches your skin.
i love the way you smile
thoughts racing, yet kept within.
i love the way your eyes take
every movement in.
i love the way you stare
at my lips, my eyes, then back again.

i love the way you grab my face before kiss—
tighten your grip against my hair, my edges, my hips.
i love the way you taste
when your tongue touches my lips.

the way you hold back, your respectfulness.
i love the way you let me climb on top,
the way you wrap your arms around me,
fingers melting down my lower back.

i love the way my breath escapes me
as your lips move across my skin,
the way my body **crumbles** like a pastry
as your hands caress me in innocence.
i love the way i wake in the morning,
dripping and begging
for one more second.

you may not remember me,
but **i remember you.**
this lifetime, the last, the many—
broken moments of heaven infinitely between us.
you were surely one of my first loves.
maybe it was better heaven split us up,
or maybe we are just drifting—
energies amongst time,
subtle moments we find within each life
where we come just close enough
to touch one another's light.

your skin melts into my figure,
fingers drip against **my thighs**.

it's like you were **written** for me.

the silhouette of my skin
projected upon the bed
beneath you.
your body on top of mine,
my breath becomes heavy,
elegantly steady
you are inside
me,
slowly
unraveling.
i lose touch with your gaze,
as my eyes roll back and my soul becomes
one with our body—
unleashed access for you to see all
of me.

everyone says that when you know,
you know.
there is no question.
no beg within your system for more
not a part of your soul that wonders
if there is an essence out there
cosmically awaiting your chance to merge-
there's no hint of gravitating in a direction,
in any opposition to your person.
there is no virtual reality within your mind,
no dreams of a time or life where your person
isn't exactly who they are in this current time,
and you feel a sense of intimate awe
in that there is a soul so purely
with you,
so real
in the sense of humanity around you
that in the moments you sit in absolution
you realize the inadequate comprehension
of a presence with more depth
than even this moment-
of a presence so worthy of you.

you eradicate me.
it's this endless wave
of becoming and **unbecoming**
ultimate humanity
expressing itself
through me.
your eyes are luminescent,
coded by caramel and ocean tides;
your chin and lips rubble,
so intricate against mine-
you feel endless
when you kiss me.

no one else makes sense
the way you do.

i just want you. to **weep** into my bones all that has been undone so i may hold you again. to drench my skin in the liquid silk of your kisses, your lips, the dust that falls from your tongue as you speak monologues to me. to allow me to listen. to allow me to witness the breath of your being, your essence, in silence.

i just want you to know that i am here, resting in my space until the day you fall upon your knees and whisper to me-
i just want you.

THE TASTE OF SKIN

i've never had anyone touch me the way you do.
i know that's common terminology often said to you,
but the way your energy comes through-
your hands against my skin,
the way you breathe into my movements-
i feel your energy in these moments,
the way you give without any attachment.

that first eve i was with you, i felt in awe
that i ever really knew you,
because this version of you
is like someone from a book-
one of those guys written into the storyline
to showcase radical love,
moments of an unconditional one.

the irony in all this is infinite.

before i ever really knew you,
i used to write erotic explorations between us-
maybe the scene was another timeline,
but i saw you in my mind's eye
and my body soaked in your skin.
and this was back when we were just friends,
soulmates or **twin flames** or
just existing particles of heaven.
i never dreamt truth into a future with you,
or that you'd be the first in an age-old fight
against my sexuality to bring me to my knees
in intimacy, and willingly.

you are **something else**

the thought of you
s o a k s
this fabric
between my legs,
my body enamored
by the idea
of your hands
upon my frame.
your lips against my skin,
my tongue glides
down your abdomen,
the softest skin
against my breath,
l i q u i d s
salivate behind my lips.

can you love me when i'm naked,
when we finally taste breath again
at the end of our sweetest expression,
wrapped in one another,
our essence untethered?

can you love me in the morning,
when my eyes are tainted with
the shadow of darkness from the
leftover mask of beauty that i painted?

can you love me from a distance,
when i'm halfway across the world,
our only connection a device
that can only listen?

can you love me when i'm faded,
when my words become a blur and
my eyes can't seem to focus on
anything in particular?

can you love me when i'm escaping,
when my body grows cold,
my mind lost in translation?

can you love me when i love you—
when i pull at every string,
unearth the things you've never seen,
when i show you a love so profound
you've never allowed it
to touch every part of your soul?

can you love me when there's nothing left,
when our bodies return to dust,
and we take our last breath?

because i can love you through all of it,
in every moment, in every step.
the real question is—

have we dropped our shadows and
lived in our truth enough,
to fall so deeply into this
that there's never another tomorrow.

rather, moments of existence
where there is only ever present bliss.

how does one girl write so much **poetry**
timid for the taste of your lips

i don't usually do this. **fall in love**, that is. but my triggers dissolve when you're in my presence, and suddenly it's like there's never been anything holding me back. i want to touch you, love you, feel you, grace your skin with my tongue. i want all of this, and usually i'm on self-destruct mode. usually, my body hardens, and sex is like tight skin and running through the motions, just wanting to know the other had a good experience. usually, i'm the cherry tart on the counter- the one you want, but once you've got her, she's gone, and the taste left in your mouth isn't creamy like crème brûlée would be. usually, i'm the one who lets others fall in love with me, and then i'm off. my heart and breath stop, and boredom creeps into my skin. out the door i have been before you even tried to get to know me. but you, you make me want to talk. i could spend hours in bed with you, just kissing and laughing and staring, and this is what scares me. part of caring about someone is knowing there's a risk they could hurt you in some way, and i'm open to that risk with you. these are the words you shared with me when i told you my faults. i don't usually do this. allow myself to be patient enough to fall in love.

touch never felt like rust to you. any day, anytime, i'll give to you,
she whispered across the room towards her lover.
i've never understood.
how could it be so easy for you to fold for them?
give and give and give and give and
i do love to feel them against my skin,
hear their breath move like an instrument by my tongue.
but never have i felt i could hand myself over in any moment
the way you do. and sometimes i wonder what love would feel like
had those moments in my mind never happened.
would i love more like you do?
be the woman everyone dreams of, available for pleasure upon a
tug of a string? the woman a rusted touch has crafted inside me
has the essence of a warrior. making love is a game of strategy:
open and receive only when they never see it coming
for only then does the moment honour my body.
sometimes
i wish i could be the woman you are.
but the lover within me is unique.
i may not be made for just anyone
and the rarity of my existence,
of my choice to surrender to love,
makes each time i welcome touch a sentence in my history book.
it's not easy for me—it's an opportunity to accept.
i cannot fall into the wish to be made differently,
for the devil feels no pity. but my soul does wonder,
did i want to love like this?
for everyone i dance with teaches me more
about trusting once again. for you it's simply
pleasure. for me it's
a war,
a dance,
victory,
illusion,
strategy,
grief, and

surrender.
each time history is made for my body while i rupture
the concept of what was done to me by recoding what i am able to do.
ride my partner like the priestess i have always been. but that day
will not be the best sex i've ever had-it will be a reclamation of my
body.
a signed contract that what had once been taken from me is now
my own again. and maybe after that, love will finally fall
unburdened from my tongue the way yours does. or
maybe i didn't come here to love the way you do.
maybe i came here to fall in love
in a way you never would. for the explorer sees things
a businessman never may. losing one thing opens a doorway
to the unknown-one you never would have walked through
had you not had to walk the other way to begin with.
had touch never rusted my skin, i wouldn't have found new ways to
love someone. this unconditional ability to give love
shows up in ways not material. i'm something else.
not human per se.
but a lover made by becoming
a warrior.

time without you feels like smoke against my lungs
and i'm not much of a smoker. until recently.
blue lotus makes my dreams speak to me, and rarely,
i find you there. never real. something about the silence
between us makes me feel like a sinner soaked in cold blood.
my mother tongue, begging for understanding
of this distance, cascades this inner dialogue.
but the answer beats against my bones, tender.
lack of love shows up like a ghost and whisks its pretty silks
against your glass before it shatters. stationed silence
beats like tension in my mind. love letters written in tongue,
cryptic codes. you'll never admit it, but what we felt
felt way too good. and here i am left
with **withering bones**-*how could i have been so wrong?*
the memory of your eyes in mine sinks into my skull.
i wasn't. sometimes what's treated like gold
is hidden away in a drawer out of sour protection
from lack of courage to wear it into open sea.
for the ocean is known to dance upon your body the way god does,
and leave you naked, missing jewelry.

maybe i was never meant to understand you. my mind's
been racing, tasting the diversity of the palate
of your energies and never have i come back
to a similar one i've felt before. you're the first
i've felt mirror me in such a dramatic way. the essence
of you reminds me of the ways i've never truly been
understood and maybe i was never meant to. understand you
or be understood, maybe we're unpalatable as beings.
maybe i should have let you be tasted in presence more deeply.
but the flavour only lasted so long before it transformed
and made me feel cold. heat flashes against my skin
by the memory of you and my heart feels wrapped in melancholy
for what i may never again experience with you. it's odd,
because i was there, more present than i've ever been
whilst exploring you, and yet it feels like it will
never be enough. you were someone i could have dove
into forever and never felt like i knew you. or possibly
it was a facade, a reflection like so much of the rest of you,
but something in my heart says otherwise. i feel lost
in translation between these **feelings and flavorings.**
missing the sweet taste of your soul.
maybe you were always meant to be
experienced and never re-explored.

HIM.

you are **an anomaly**
he says to me over and over again.
nobody has ever been everything with me,
both communicably and emotionally,
sexually and cosmically,
two sides of the same stone
and yet here
you are
right in front
of me.

let me tell you,
i dreamt of a man last night.
his sweet hands were inside me, and he said,
he didn't want to fuck me—
not yet.
he watched me,
elixir gliding down his hand,
tracing the back of my legs.
breathy kisses against his lips,
i provided.
look me in the eyes, he said,
don't look away—not even at your last breath.
i want to watch you unfold for me,
to trust that i'll pleasure you before
you ever let me have you.
let me tell you,
i dreamt of a man last night—
one who surpassed the dreams i allow myself to have
outside of my physical reality.
he taught me to accept only a letter of love
etched into my skin by his tongue,
dancing across my lips
with no expectation of return.
i dreamt of a man last night.
he reminded me what it feels like
to be wealthy in love.
so i mapped his love
and devoured every inch of him.

THE TASTE OF SKIN

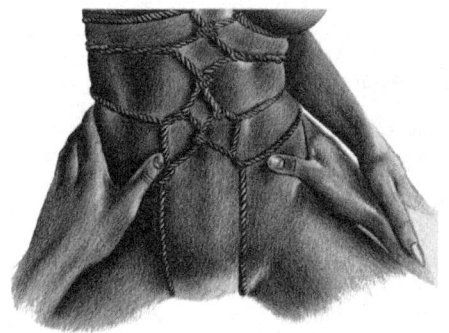

let him play you,
let him play with you,
let him play with every edge of your skin,
your mouth,
your mind,
your heart.
because if he's already playing you,
then why not let yourself be touched
the way **instruments** were meant to be?
allow the frequency of your love
to vibrate from you.
the sounds he will emit from you
will touch each and everyone
in ways you never would've felt had he not
traced his tongue down the spine of your cords
and shown you what it means to be love.
so be love.

do you trust me? he asks.
a nod and smirk against my lips.
his hands twist my body across his,
flipped backwards upon him,
our hips oppositely directed and yet
intimately in alignment.

lay your chest against the bed and
just relax, he says.
my legs straddled across his hips;
all of my being vulnerably candlelit.
one of his hands rests upon my lower back
while the other explores
inside my skin. my breath heavy
as his energy echoes vibrations
throughout my system, the mysterious vessel of a woman.
i can feel his presence,
each movement a motion of intuition,
and my hips match his rhythm,
pulsations wrapping his silken fingertips.
moments elongate as my breath escapes,
denser with every second,
the release-unended.
my lips lightly gracing the sheets upon the bed,
losing control of my grip
as moans expel from my lips.
each thought in my head, repetitive:
i've never felt something like this.

my heart beats inside my skull,
shadows slither in my peripheral.
she feels like the sun—
rays of **bursting heaven**—
deep within my body.
she glistens as he melts into her.

speak to me in french, i beg.
my eyes tilt toward his,
our naked bodies lie next to one another,
the sweetness of our skin colliding again,
j'ai encore plus envie de te **baiser**.
his deep eyes lock with mine—
my soul aches for his breath,
my tongue salivates for translation,
a smile creeps upon my lips.
i want to fuck you once more.
this time, he insists.

j'ai envie de vous faire **l'amour**,
the ocean sang to the sun.
the tides whispered
as the evening light hung;
each morning, the sun would wander
his rays along each wave
of the ocean's tongue.

THE TASTE OF SKIN

your lips are soaked in the taste of my skin,
your tongue unmasked by our kiss-
a pause for my breath
against your neck-
saliva thick upon my breasts.

whispers exchanged between licks,
moans held in my chest,
time reminds me
to leave again—
he sees thoughts walk beyond my mind.

you can stay a little longer, he sighs,
you've stated your boundaries,
i will not cross them, he smiles.
desire unfolds as he slowly kisses my chest,
a breath escapes me-
your **respect** is dismantling.

teeth compress against my bottom lip.
your hips against mine-
your hands, the perfect fit-
as if they were made for **a handful of my skin**.
i want you
like this,
for a moment longer than our kisses provide.

revelations in each ritualistic movement,
intimacy speaks through my tongue.
she reminds me what it means to be love,
to worship the soul,
to wield the sword of infinite energy
as i beg for him
to moan my name in ecstasy.

and so his soul said to mine,
have you noticed our dance across life
these conversation through time
are the only findings we have
more intricate than the **delicate pages** of a book?

i don't know how to integrate
the moments i've had with you.
one soft and sweet,
tender movements
of hands and body
wrapped all up around me.
the next, jumbled,
loving one another for reasons
we can't put into words—
our communication scattered,
simply because we desire one another
in a way that may never be.
we've been friends for so long
that i imagined laughter—
naked in bed,
sprawled across your chest,
finally getting to watch you tell me a story.
the laughter upon your lips,
red wine in the cracked edges,
your words revealing parts of you
i had never seen before.
i finally got to see him—
that man i knew i was in love with.
but somehow, i don't know you,
just him, maybe from another lifetime
or lineage of moments.
but we've sat in a room,
crowded by frequency and yet
nobody was there
but you and i.
our souls have something within them—
unfathomable not to long for their connection,
and yet still isn't yet time.
maybe the concept of our alignment
is something meant to be unkept.
i don't know you,
but i do miss him.

       | my **forbidden**.

i see that side of you.
i do not hate him, nor do i love him,
but i understand why he exists within you.
he is not the man i want; he is a mere fraction
of your soul i call into mine.
he is not all of you. and i want you to know this,
because i know you see it too, in the mirror,
when you stare back at yourself
too late into the night,
fueled by **too many bottles** of wine.
i desire so much more of you.
i pray you release this facade,
the one you've wrapped around the depths of you,
so you may realign with the best of you.
so you may call for god's soul, too.

THE TASTE OF SKIN

I want to be inside you,
he whispers against my ear.
his tongue slides over my neck,
plants slow kisses across my collarbone,
his mouth a compass
moving down my chest.

hands lock into mine
hold my body against the bed—
his smile an invitation
to watch his pleasure in this.

my breath heats against his movement.

he pulls himself back toward my kiss,
moves his tongue across my lips,
let me make love to you
he **offers** again.

his blue-speckled eyes envelop mine.
the thoughts in his mind, i cannot devise.
a smirk insinuates i may be a light in his life.
what a gift the heavens have bestowed upon me—

to be a channel between spirit and **his smile**.

THE TASTE OF SKIN

my body melts into yours
the way water seeps into sand:
it's there one minute and the next—
one essence remains, grains lightly wet.
the softness of you and i exists
and yet expands.
one moment sweet,
our kisses heaven-sent—
the next, your grip is tough,

calloused fingers inside my skin,
the shower hot and heavy,
yet you lift me toward the edge,
my breath echoing into the open evening,
shadows of palm trees the scene at hand.
you ask me to trust you.
i'm not sure if i'm ready yet.

i laughed,
and then he bit my lip.
our kisses were lightning.
my tongue slid against his.
eat me, i teased.
and he did.

THE TASTE OF SKIN

he smells like liquid smoke and whiskey
but all **he drinks** is me.

THE TASTE OF SKIN

i want my tongue to slide across your skin and taste
the fragrance you emit.
i want to kiss **every**
i
n
c
h
of you.
i want you to grab my hips, match my rhythm to your breath,
sweet milky textures soaking the cloth
between our bodies.
i want you to slide your fingers between my lips,
the woman in me coats your skin,
as you invite yourself inside me.
listening to my breath, heavy against your lips.
i want you to tighten your grip,
watch my body match your kiss,
your other hand on the back of my hips,
our eye contact heavy and helpless.
kiss me
bite me
take me
i want you
inside me—
i want you to grace my body with yours.
softly into me, our breaths enlightened
by the first moments of this sacred interconnected energy.
you have me
in this moment
eternally.

he drank the tides from my tongue,
the **silk from my skin**.
heaven walked through each of our vessels-
a tender love i hadn't experienced
until this.

whispers of kisses
against the edges
of my abdomen,
liquid from the heavens
a monsoon
collected in the crevices
of my skin,
a hollow breath
escapes my chest,
s   l   o   w   l   y,
as i breathe him in.

honey, he said.
**every square
inch** of your
essence.

THE TASTE OF SKIN

i can taste you,
he says to me.
3000 miles + an ocean between our words,
and yet the memory of his tongue against me
is more vivid than my last evening of dreams.

tu me manques.

you are missing from me.

THE TASTE OF SKIN

i love the way he feels on my skin,
soft fingertips activate my vessel—
this is **l u c i d**.
do you dream of your hands
against the tender plains of my chest?
or is it me experiencing you,
tapped into another timeline?
her heart beats in my chest.

i want to wake to sweet and soft kisses against the back of my shoulders, my neck, breakfast fed to my lips. i want to laugh about the moment, turn to my person and kiss them. i want to make love to each other, echoes of our breath filling the room. our energy so arousing that i was already soaked before they placed their fingers between my legs to play. before i begged for more of them, and even then,

    wait, you said, sliding your face down my waist, your tongue a pick,
playing **melodies** with the guitar of my clit.
i can't hold back, i call your name,
my body erupting in vibration. *finally*,
pulling you to my face,
climbing,
melting into you.
our souls, one again.

if you and i were to intertwine today then i'd melt some chocolate in a pan since it is valentine's day. there would be strawberries and banana halves resting on the edge, awaiting our hands to caress them softly with **chocolate** drippings. we'd watch the liquid cling to the skin of the fruit, sweetly hardening to show us each and every detail of their body, and i'd arrange them, perfectly imperfect coated masterpieces, upon a tray. into the freezer they'd stay for the time needed, and in those moments i would need you. need you to lick the chocolate off my neck and breasts from us painting topless. need you to let me trace your chest in kisses and lead you to our bed. laughter as we'd trip against the floor and fall over onto one another. linen sheets against our skin as our tongues made love our lips couldn't get enough. soft and slow movements. heavy breaths relinquished. your hands inside me as i tilt backwards against your body, your fingers laced in this silk of mine, and my tongue traveling against your abdomen, v line, your cock hard against my lips as i welcome you in my mouth. your hands begin to match the rhythm of my lips as you move in and out, my tongue twisting against your skin, your fingers inside and softly gracing my light. i can feel this heat rising in my body and back into you. my hand matches the rhythm of my mouth, back and forth against you, you whisper "get on top of me" as i pull my lips from your skin and twist onto you. slowly you walk yourself inside me, and our breath matches as we enter one another. the rest is ancient history, because at this point you completely eradicate me, erotically and fantastically.

heartbreak brings me to **life.**

his tongue graces my lips,
salivated by dewdrops of this
elixir i made **just for him**.

late at night, i laid in bed,
whispers in the back of my head—
did he ever even love you?
stop that, my heart snaps back-
what matters is that you loved him.
you laid all of you out on the floor
and said everything you had within.
you set your beating heart in your hands
and held it out for him
with **skylit tears** of the purest light.
you asked him, would you care for this?
the answer never mattered
because you did it-
you opened yourself again.
the part of you that had hardened,
that thick shield of ice
wrapped around your heart,
has finally softened.
your warmth has reignited
and you've let your heart beat again.
love was deeply felt no matter his feelings,
and that is your accomplishment.
now, my darling, you know
that you can do it over again.
my love, you have found
yourself through this.

i never saw a future with you.
i saw intimacy, an unexpected pregnancy—
thankfully, one that never came to life.
your sister and i, as friends,
exchanging random messages
through time, of her presence in my life,
but never yours.
i never saw where we'd be in three years,
or three weeks—
all i ever saw was presence,
and i only ever felt how lucky i was
in the moments you were right in front of me, baring
the love we shared, the intimacy we felt.
i could've seen all that as a red flag.
i could've added it to the mix
of things that just weren't—
the reasons we'd never make it.
but instead, i felt and received all of it as a gift.
us never making it kept me so present
that every single moment was one more i'd been given,
one more i could hold as sweet reminiscence
of the untold love story of you and me.
i turned a timid time into a reckoning.
i may have never seen a future with you, but
i did see everything you and i could be separately.
i did see a friendship across time,
of us silently rooting for each other.
it brings tears to my eyes, the love
i will forever have for you,
and a gift into my life,
the way i will remember you—
my **once upon a time**.

i find myself **swallowing** my tongue when it comes to you.
i find my body vain in desire for your lips against mine.
the ache of my heart beats like it did from the moment i met you,
and it has yet to cease.
you even haunt my daydreams.
one moment, it's someone who fills every desire i crave,
and the next, your face fills the hallways within my mind.
are you dreaming of me?
speaking of me?
thinking of me?
where are these visions coming from?
because if they are not from you,
then they are simply of me.
my tongue chokes its way down my throat
at the thought of you, for i am still unsure
of what this life may offer me without you.
i may find it—real love, someone who honors me—
but in choosing myself now, to find that,
to walk away from this burning within my skin,
this echo of a razor slicing my wrists,
this endless ache for you and i to be one—
am i abandoning myself also?
am i walking away from something so alive
that i may never feel my skin breathe for another's again
in the way i do for you?
i often remember, above every moment, the way
your body melted into mine, and mine into yours.
your hands fit my skin, traced my wrists,
and though your heart wept for more than i could provide,
i still wanted to hold you.
i wanted to watch you manifest and receive everything
you wanted in life. and after empty words and unkept promises,
i still yearn to see that for you.
i've never loved one so dear to pray for their absolution
the way i have for you since the day you left.
for the question that beckons me now:
is it love or apathy that activates
these depths of me?
in this ache from you,
am i falling more towards what is meant for me,
or denying myself a love that awakens me?

sometimes missing you feels
like every cell in my body is falling,
the gravitational pull of earth has suddenly
been enhanced by three—
my knees and elbows were made for the floor,
the system of walls and tunnels inside me thicken,
and my breath becomes intimately dense.
tears begin to exist and drench my skin,
all of me is lost to the heaviness and
i don't even feel like me—
but that's because i am not;
rather i am this simplistic existing particle
and if i were placed beneath a microscope
between two little glass sheets,
all you would see is the genetic makeup
of a druggie—
addicted to the most epic of highs,
a love that is never good for me.
and yet, i still find moments where the pull is so deep
that i see you
as if you're still in my reality,
as if you never left me—
our bodies melting into one another
i'm up on my kitchen counter and
your hands are making me sing a breathy choir,
filling my home with this desire
i've always dreamed of.
the last time i touched myself
i felt your hands inside me,
the memory of your skin warm against mine
and our kisses, i could barely handle it—
my body expelled in ecstasy by thought:
this is the type of addiction that robs your heart.
you're so intimate inside your mind that
the following moment is unleashed heaviness,
your back upon the floor,

heaven has walked through your body
and you can only dream of the day
someone else may finally touch you—
and yet you wonder,
will it ever be the same?
will it be better?
or will i miss you for eternity?
this addiction isn't very healthy of me,
and yet, sometimes missing you feels heavenly.
sometimes **missing you** fills me in ways
that may one day bring me true ecstasy—
because these memories i see
are only of the moments you eternally
devoured me.

you could've been an **asshole**
a thousand times over,
and yet still the most real lover
i'd ever let into my life.

and that's why the princess falls
for the bad guy before the prince-
the honesty.
brutally beautiful, a tragically unfiltered
love story to teach the truth of longevity.
to teach her how to serve and not serve
her cravings of safety, depth,
and unbred kin.

FREYA RAY

i never realized how much i desired
until i had you.

it's been **11 months** since i fell in love with you.
that's 334 days, 8,030 hours, or 481,800 minutes
of memories of you leaning over my shoulder,
teaching me how to be more human.

it's been 11 months since i fell in love with you,
and i still find myself tumbling upon the floor,
in heartbreak, my voice bellowing to the elders
that things never worked out with you,
that i had to choose to walk away from you—
prayers against the sky that another love may come,
one that sets me on fire the way you did,
honors me alive, and craves me like i did you.

it's been 11 months since i actually fell in love with you.
took 36 months before the day i realized i wanted you,
and by then i was a distant soul,
your new girl telling me all the ways
i was but a small flame
keeping you warm on your way home to her.

it's been 48 months since the day i met you.
that's 1,460 days, 35,000 hours, or 2,102,000 minutes.
the first time i saw you,
i thought you were just another one of them—
these men in our crew on an egocentric climb.
but then our eyes met, and for the first time in my life,
i felt that electricity that sparks the flame within.

intensity as the days moved forward,
and i couldn't touch you,
but every muscle in my being
pulled me closer toward you.
each year ached for me to be with you—
until the moment i was.

at first, it was everything it wasn't meant to be:

hard, overdone, disconnected, and wrong.
but then it was soft, lucid, and elevating.
the fire within reclaimed me,
and you awoke a numbing, activated this realm
of ecstasy that has reset everything.
without you, i wouldn't know
the most honest truths of my being.
as simply as i can say it,
you've rewritten me.

it's been 11 months since the day i fell in love with you,
7 months since the day you told me you'd been cursed
to believe you'd pass in your mid-30s. but i've lost before,
and i trusted you to a degree that my heart shattered that day,
so i walked away by letting you.

and yet, my heart still pounds at the thought of you.

2,102,977 minutes since i met you,
and you're still a blueprint that whispers to my soul.
i pray to move on from you, but
the hardest truth of all is that i may never.
for now, all i can see is the

unknown.

THE TASTE OF SKIN

all i miss sometimes is the mark of your hand

in mine.

THE TASTE OF SKIN

i am delicate these days
especially in the wake of
books and men

THEY.

thank you.
thank you.
thank you.
thank you.
thank you.

sometimes there comes a reckoning-
when the illusion before you
suddenly dissipates into truth.
the part of you that could see
any and all possibilities fades
and the facade of what was this illustrious love,
this one-of-a-kind story,
evaporates.
you're left watching these memories
dance before your eyes
and the energy you felt within them
is a distant history.
the love you experienced becomes
the kind in books and movies,
the kind you remember
but cannot understand why it ever happened
because it was,
in the subtlest of terms,
a dichotomy.
it's as if you've hit the point against time
where there is no return of this feeling.
you've approached the moment
between one timeline and the next,
and it feels like freedom
and yet
it also feels like **the end.**
and yet
it is said over and again,
where one story ends
another must always begin.

look at these **waves**,
the ways they move and mold,
the way they topple upon themselves.
they thrive through seasons of intensity,
and yet still,
they find moments of serenity. days
between winter's swells, centered energy
in a season of madness. they are always
malleable, never confined to the
restraint of what lies before them.
instead, they melt into a mass,
becoming a new artistic
phenomenon,
just for a single moment
to pass. eternally transferring
their energy, they shift the world
around them into something new—
something never before seen,
always changing.

i know you'll never know this,
but you'll sit next to my heart with hands upon mine,
a tether splayed on the cutting board before us,
forever teaching me
how to spell chemistry with a knife.

i know you'll never know this,
but our love will run through my veins like these days
i spend tickling my divine spine with medicines
i shouldn't have access to-**and** still you
will **always** be the one i can't get rid of.
the heavens remind me of you.

i know you'll never know this,
but your heart will beat next to me for a lifetime
to come, beyond one, and into the time of energy.

often i wonder if all i was in your life
was a listener.
no matter-
what a gift it was
to listen
to you.

it's like we never actually happened.
and yet the print of your soul against my energy
system seems to be **singed-**
if i listen,
i can still feel your heart
beat inside mine.

love is a dirty, filthy, beautiful thing.
some say she destroys you;
some say she sets your free.
well, in what i've witnessed of myself
these past few eternal weeks,
she's reclaimed herself within a part of me
i had forgotten knew how to breathe.
she grew through my system,
a newly born vine weaving herself
within in my blood stream
and now i feel like those **paintings**-
the ones gently crafted by broken fingertips
and unpainted nails.
the ones like a replica
of women, the earth growing through their bones;
the ones where you know
she wasn't born with a plates of mastery
handed to her upon a throne,
but rather rags and whispers
of the story of an age-old soul,
the history we now write into books,
the story buried amongst stories,
the legend of the one who has to soften her roots
in the worst of times to be
and be
and become
again,
something so new
that paintings are born
from it.

the way i dream of the day you arrive
upon my doorstep-
a soft knock
followed by a hollow opening
for the silence of the moments
and **words you left unsaid**
fills the space between us.
our hearts both shattered,
and yet newly activated.
hey, you whisper with soft eyes
as you witness my breath.
a timid hi escapes my lips
before we fall into one another's kiss
like time never stopped existing
and the energy picked up
exactly where we left it.

originally, i thought i could only
write about heartbreak,
or say
the breaking
of my own trust,
because i'd only ever let myself love
one who would eventually combust.
it was a shallow escape,
one i knew i could embrace
without being seen
as the one who ended things.
i thought eventually
i'd end up alone.
i always felt safe there.
i couldn't manage to take the one step
that would strengthen my own depth-
the movement that would tell me
if i was actually meant for someone.
i constantly found a trailhead already run
such heavy pockets in the ground
that sometimes it wasn't even fun.
but i always saw the one in my peripheral-
the trail that was paved
with long strands of grass
bent over by the last person
who dared take the track
most others wouldn't.
i remember the first time my dad
took me off-roading,
i felt the world expand
as i found life others didn't have.
he always made new **trailheads**.
and so here i am,
at the edge of these tall blades of grass,
with my trailhead
yet molded,
and my journey set
to unfold.

ive done it once again-
woken up drenched in your skin.
you taught me what love really is.
you taught me to listen to the winds
and feel **the earth** beneath my feet.
what it feels like to breathe in another's frequency.
you taught me the love that sets you free
is the kind where you show up for me
and i appreciate however that may be,
and i show up for you and
you have no expectation of how that may be.
we ebb and flow within each other's worlds
and we exist together and yet so individually
i t ' s   p o e t i c .
when i touch you, the energy releases from me
and you transmute it once again into synergy.
i feel you cry with me and laugh with me
and we sit in awe of silence and beauty together.
all these lessons you have shared just by being together,
with one another. we merge in moments and in most
we echo back to one another these new things we have learned.
my love for you is this golden token in representation
of the love we all deserve.
one of unity and presence and simply
existence.

you used to say to me that deep down
you felt we were meant to be—
that one day we'd be something.
and in the wake of those words,
the hopes you'd felt so deeply and yet
never actually stood upon,
i'd like to say a few things.
firstly, i never believed you—
or of us one day becoming something.
yet, the concept you fed me of a futuristic reality of us
swept me up so i fell in love with this idea
of being nothing.
i used to believe i was in love with you,
and i was, but the honest truth is that i loved the part of me
that never had to commit to anything,
that could simply be in a moment
and make these decisions of wild intimacy
and never anything of longevity—
i felt so free that i fell in love with being.
in the wake of this hope,
this conceptualized epitome of love,
the existential crisis taught me i actually want
something sustainable.
i've now fallen for a long-lost triumph
of realizing i want someday to be something –
tangible,
physical,
visible atoms in front of my eyes.
i want more than a concept
and only in this hope of you and i,
this unknown predicament,
have i found the reality of desire,
of wanting something real—
something more than delicate words.
a desire to represent as the epitome
of an epic love that is known, certain.
one that is not of two magnets
repelled by the void between us,
but is undeniable by the cognizance
of **nothing but us.**

THE TASTE OF SKIN

do you still think of me?
because i see you in so many of my dreams
or maybe my subconscious is speaking to me.
maybe the **subtleties** of my love for you
are still vibrating through me
and manifesting themselves
through my dreams.

what a rare occurrence it is to write of someone
and the words never cease to represent
every second you bled into my essence.
dancing liquids we were. how blessed.

say eradicate my bones
from their limbs
say erode the shackles between love and
i
say
erase the lines that we know as us
fill them in with illusions of
lust and love
say exclamations of **her**oic temptations
say electricity is what i feel when you're in
my energy, my being, my dreams, my everything
say to me anything, say everything, say her.

why is it that **god named you** so poetically
and i am here, tears upon my writings,
unable to share god's giving.

i still love you.
i still miss your soft touch upon my skin.
i had never had anyone touch me
the exact way i wanted to be touched
until you did. even the simple way you held my breasts
or slid your fingers down my neck.
i always felt like heaven sent you to me.
but then,
watching you walk away
from a love as deep as this
shattered me.
i couldn't really understand
in the beginning
because all i could see was all of me
upon the floor, the flood of love within me
seeping through the parts of me
still holding the thought of you so deeply
and i was **the tarot's tower**—
rebirth was all that was left for me.
the structure of love in my head needed a new blueprint
to be sturdy once again, this time cemented within
by a frequency of worthiness.
and i did find it.
only now that my tower is built
by internal power and breath
can i see how intimately i loved you.
and i understand now.
why it is that our hearts truly break.
it wasn't as much the ache of you walking away
but the part of me that silenced
my ability to love you even if you didn't stay.
if a love is true it never really does go away.
and it feels so good to love you
again today.

i felt your hands between my thighs,
your fingers intertwined in my being.
you pulled my hand,
guided my fingers alongside yours,
teaching me the soft movements
of these textures within.
right here,
you whispered,
play with this.
this moment, one of my deepest lessons,
the perfect reminisce.
| he taught me

because right now it's your move.
and my love, the only way for you to make it
is to keep healing. **rise**.
rise with yourself and then come find me.
and if you do, i will be there,
where the stars align.
i will be here waiting for you.

the **strength** you have built within me
                    | radiance

i always felt you were my end-all,
but it was never you.
the years we spent drenched in a million echoes-
tapestries of words writing the love story
we'd one day fall into through memories alone.
the days we spent wrapped in one another's skin,
hands to my chest, my face lucid for you
meiomi our golden token
my still skin bare.
i always felt you were my end because you knew-
knew me in ways nobody had ever seen
when i'm the one who sees everything-
every dark corner, these prophetic dreams,
the space between one's chains upon the floor
and their hands clenched around the key,
the bottom of their tongue tasting of rust,
the stories they expel to me in memory,
and for once I felt you saw me the ways I saw-
subconsciously we are keys to ourselves
and i thought you were mine.
i thought you could unlock my divinity.
tall strands of grass as i lie amongst them
dissolve into moths, willows sing to me
it was never you.

i always felt you were my end,
but it was a projection
of all i have ever been meant to be
reflecting back at me-
you were always a kaleidoscope.
a gift to me so eternally still
and always differently than I had dreamt.
i always felt you were my end
because **you were mine**-or of me-
but it was never you.
blue - red - violet - a midnight's sky.
i was my end. and you were simply my eyes.

it's illustrious the way i fall for words,
beg for more, and ache at the letters
you use to fool me.
what gracious curves-
and i said thank you.

                         | **a poet's eulogy**

for how could i have known
that you were more than the simple
love of my life
but **a keeper** of a blueprint,
one of the keys to my internal system,
a coded invitation-once entered,
activated and remembered,
forever implemented-
erotic pleasures.

she is the embodiment of love,
the cruel witness to the most epic of moments,
the most raw.
and once again, she is in my system—
i realize she never left.
but all snake skins must be shed
by the crisp, unforgiving sword of a broken heart.
oh, to shift and turn in steady unrest,
to beg for surrender once again,
to crave to feel **her heart**
beat through your chest.

hope was the killer that nobody warned me existed-
she sat on her throne and burnt me into pieces.
and in my wake, i accepted no fate
for there was nothing left to burn.
there was no expectation
to live up to anymore.
the castle walls finally began to disintegrate
and as they fell away like dust in the wind,
there you were-
like i had held myself in and away from love
because i trusted too much in ideas-
that weren't even mine.
it's as if by letting go
of that existence
heaven finally gifted me with
a piece of divinity
after all this time
and i finally get to
walk towards you

i sat myself upon you as my throne
bones born for bones
heat incinerates our souls as we merge.
third eyes aside, this is a reclamation of

                                                    self.

my spinal chord bends time as
cracks move up my porcelain skin.
you've granted me the opportunity to shatter.
your hands grasp my hips,
a gravitational dance made of erotic elegance renders,
liquid fire burns its way through my system
as the knots once purged into my womb
become unwritten.

                                    | i, **woman**, am born.

change is inevitable, they'd say
change will find you and devour little pieces
until a day comes where you look at the sweetness
that once was and barely recognize it.
but the form it takes now is so enticing-
caramel flows down your edges
and somehow now you're in love with it.
She's still made of the same presence
but takes on this world like someone you've never seen
before, a hidden soul that once lay dormant within you,
a livelihood of recognition born from within.

THE TASTE OF SKIN

my tongue soft, swift,
exploring the imprints of my fingertips.
the tang of vinegar clings to my lips,
my cheeks swell with a peppery kick.
my throat opens, welcoming within
this perfectly balanced taste of heaven—
handcrafted by desire,
a touch of everything
that sets my soul on fire.
a shock **ripples** through me as i swallow,
this moment, god's service, utterly divine.

i was worried this last time
that i wouldn't find **my way back**,
after i lost myself so deeply
in every crevice of you.
yet, somehow my heart has found
a hidden beat that had never been-
a part of me so wild
that this time all i want is to devour
every second of my breathe

in honour of this human existence.

THE TASTE OF SKIN

and she is born.
released through a wicked rupture,
echoing against my lungs,
liquid silk relinquishing itself—
the leftover taste upon my tongue.
the **red hues** of my love
bleed against the pages
of a softened, reborn
love.

THE TASTE OF SKIN

the mirror used to tell me the parts of my body
that weren't meant to be mine
used to show me what it looked like
to be a girl who isn't heavy in her skin
because the breath she welcomes into her being
isn't enough to move it,
just enough to keep a tight stomach.
the mirror used not to be my friend,
and i never realized how much i've grown into my senses
until the other day when i saw myself again,
or maybe for the first time
where i actually saw my skin,
the way my legs melted into my hips
the elasticity of my breasts
as my hands would caress them,
or the way my abs would move
as a huge breath journeyed through my system,
music in my ears and my body one with the rhythm
it felt like the layers of my being, my skin, my blood,
the hallways inside me were speaking.
the mirror used to tell me things that were empty,
and now that i feel the blood coursing through my veins,
it's like the mirror actually sees all of me
every,
simple,
human,
ecstasy.

my deepest relationship has always been with her. she reminds me how deep the silence can be, and also how vulnerable. she welcomes me in with arms like none i have ever witnessed, and still, in these moments, it's as if i am being held for the first time, by a mother, by my lifeline. she echoes in my thoughts the prayers i had forgotten when i stepped into this vessel, beginning the journey of what is an active presence of learning to remember. **she licks** my being with salted kisses stripping away the energies that no longer serve me. she alchemizes instantaneously as if it's as easy as breathing, shifting the tides of the universe through light frequency. she reminds me what a gift it is to be human. to love heavenly, to breathe energy, to speak the patterns of thought between two molds of mass. she reminds me what it feels like to be one. to be everything and nothing all at once.

and one of these days someone i deeply care for will share my bed with me. the wind will still whistle through my home. an island breeze will curate a chill against each of our spines. activated desire will flow through our eyes. moans will echo through the valley as candles flicker against my walls. the smell of sandalwood will seep through the space. we will share our souls with one another through moments of presence and laughter. and **stories will walk** across our tongues. naked bodies will be wrapped in dim lighting. the muse of timeless paintings will be reborn through him and i. we will breathe in love together. and i will be held for all the dots of time forward. i will be honored and worshipped divinely and humanly-at last.

something's been **happening** within me.
these dormant, ecstatic revolutions
are reviving—you seem to have fine-tuned
my body back to the erotic evolution of humanity.

i love her. The new, the erotic, her presence, her brilliance.
but i love her too. the old her, the young her, the naked her.
i love way she elegantly walks in her skin, just her skin.
i love the way she laughs at simplicity
and deep dives into
the elements.
i love the way she embodies herself. she's always shocked me
by having the audacity to do all these little things others have so
many judgements on. and she does them because they represent so
much of who she is just on regular basis. the way she walks topless
in her house for days or sleeps in nothing and sometimes everything
but nobody knows. it can all be a persona, but the realness of her
in her skin is what radiates authenticity. it's beauty at its finest.
and as i evolve again and again and again, i hope to bring her with
me, always, never forgetting her honesty or the parts of her that
existed- because that's where all of this started. i want to remember
every step of this adventure-all the way from the beginning into
and beyond the comical end.

i'd rather have my **heart broken**.
because when i was young, i fell for it.
the chase away from love. allowing the dust
to build up within me if it could save the tragedies
i would feel, had i felt. i thought if i could just swallow
my heart well enough, it would beat
against my gut and tell me i was right to close.
the egoic tendencies that drone me gave others
the magic to alchemize, and i was left cold,
colder than before and now i crave warmth.
the kind that comes from giving in, letting my heart be held
in your hands for the sheer joy
of having faith in the unknown.
i crave the markings against my skin of your essence,
your fingertips joined, united,
because we'll heal.
but forever will our sigils be carved into one another.
that's what i want. i'd rather have my heart broken
because the symphonies that will rise through me
from a shattered energy body are what i live for.
and all the alchemy i used to hand away
becomes my own to yield. and only in heartbreak
have i told stories coated in shredded flakes of gold.

THE TASTE OF SKIN

yesterday i found myself unraveled,
my body draped across the corner of my bed,
rose quartz warm within my womb,
vibrations pulsating through my system.
yesterday i found myself heavenly again,
infinitely exploring these waves of my body,
each movement unruly to the satisfaction of my tongue.
yesterday i found myself in all of this-
because of you.
i melted against my own love,
dripping elixirs i had never known
until you touched me.
remembering those moments you showed me,
your hands guiding me against the intricacies
of my own internal skin,
textures so delicate, yet found by you.
you taught me to feel her in ways
i'd never even explored for my own joy.
yesterday i found myself begging again,
this time for a moment to tell you
how pleasurable it was for me
to learn, explore, and be
taught once again.

THE TASTE OF SKIN

imagine if i bled into your mouth,
the liquid red of **a thousand sheds** dripping
from your lips—
the screams i would emit
as your tongue graced my sacred
                                      woman's
                                                        skin.

my intimacy is filled with twists and turns-
curved edges down her back,
dividends of sand against her skin,
sweet silken juice extending past her mouth.
at times she is deep, illustrious and dark,
boldened by knots and ties teasing her skin,
wet by the icy tightness that is aching against
each of her edges. and at times she is swapped,
prickled by **a spine** filled with spikes of remembrance,
bodily renders of past times.
sometimes she even cries to the gods,
vocal eradication of a moment untimely left.
my dear intimacy is, though, rooted in gold-
flakes in time where she roars
like the sun against my skin
a few hours too long.
she is holy, erotic, naked, misunderstood,
and inflamed by a desire that could beseech her,
a tongue twisted in elevation at the pleasure
she will one day take in-
all by an erotic temptress, her kin.

THE TASTE OF SKIN

i already love you,
the **echo** of your laugh against my ear.

my dearly Beloved,
you taught me that fairytales exist. you taught me that my heart
will shatter and rebuild itself again. you taught me that i can
choose love despite how love chooses. and i love you for this.

mr.j, baby, you taught me that you can love anyone. no matter what
they've done or what they consist of, you taught me that i can fall
in love with everyone. you taught me true forgiveness. that my heart
will beat and breathe again.

my sacred union, my once upon all time, you taught me that an un-
conditional love is mine. that no matter how you move or shift, that
even if you never commune within my life again, i still get to love
you-eternally through my existence.

but you, my forbidden. well you taught me that you don't choose who
you fall in love with. you taught me that love can be given-freely.
you taught me that i can love without this resistance, that i can
open, that i can have fun with it. you reminded me that i can love you
even if you never come back to my presence. that i can let love go,
and be okay again.

and, my reflection, you taught me that i am where this begins. that
it was always about loving the one within before you could love
honestly.

and my one, my only, you're teaching me that love will find me again.
you're teaching me that love will be in the oddest of corners, that
she will come out of nowhere, wrap around your skin, and remind you
that love is all there is.

                                        | **my epic loves.**

THE TASTE OF SKIN

last night i dreamt of two beings
intermixed
only skin, the taste of lips
our bodies without distance-
it was like a few drops of the divine
were placed within each human
only to be tapped into so rarely-
an alchemical reaction of ecstasy-
and as we found that first light
where we began to dissolve between time
we evolved into stardust
and scattered ourselves across the sky.

may our **union** be one of infinite matrimony.

and **why shouldn't i?**
why shouldn't i fall madly in love with myself?
why shouldn't i make intimate eye contact with my being
as i melt under the touch of my own hands?
why shouldn't i eat a slice of that cake-
feel the chocolate fall down my lips,
my tongue swiftly there to catch it,
saliva soft against my skin,
as taste relishes itself within my mouth.
a reminder.
why shouldn't i envelop my soul in pleasure?
why shouldn't i watch my hips
match the rhythm of your lips
as you devour my essence?
why shouldn't i reckon the awakening of my body
in honor of yours, watch our humanity unravel?
listen to the echoes of our hymns fill the room,
my hands grasping onto you, the mold of my being too,
this union intimately devoured-
ecstasies unraveled.
why shouldn't i?

it's like **calligraphy**,
the clouds written against the sky.
what do you think they're saying?

do you think our angels are writing
the current chapter of our life?

your soul enthralls me
an ocean and time between us
and yet i can feel you inside me-
the way your hands will hold my body,
the back of my neck as you kiss my tongue,
our mouths soft and timid
yet untamed and erotic,
devoured moments between lust and love
this perfectly imperfect alignment of us
laughter fills the room between breath
and whispers caress our beings with
a deep remembrance
our intimacy is one of a radical love
i haven't yet experienced
and oddest of it all is the way you activate me
and we haven't even met.
these **visions** in my head of you and me,
are tidal waves. your hands explore
the depths of my matter,
a choir of my breath vibrates through us,
and you whisper in my ear
that you only want us.

i ache for the day you are physical
and not solely in my third eye.
tu me manques, **mon amor**, my life.

i want to feel you radiate
symphonies of **vibrations**,
dancing into the skies,
powerful liquidation,
soaking the fabric of my light-
may i feel one with the witness
of this intimate timeline.

it's an odd feeling to fall in love with someone
you don't even know yet,
but **the phoenix** twisted my view
as she emerged within me,
as if that death was the first death
that finally outgrew me,
and i awoke free
to walk naked across this land.
for there are no more castle walls
when you kill the soldier
rather than the man.

i don't know you yet,
but i can hear **your voice**
singing against my skin.
vibrations of these moments unkept,
whispers of a love only my bones knew
was near.
i already love you, my dear.
i patiently wait for the day we may mend,
until the day you remind me
of the memory my heart has been holding:
the taste of your skin.

the day i meet you will be subtle. soft and timid like the sounds of a whistling bird against the horizon of rain. loud and distant but close and instant all in the same. the day i meet you will be like any other day, with an added smile and a lilting laugher in my veins. as if its already happened- as if we've met in a million seconds in **a million frames.**

i want to make love to you,
s/he says.

tea soaked paper and **red ink,**
i kind of think you were meant for me.

take me.
save me.
elevate me.
show me.
behold me.
teach me.
shower me.
worship me.
remind me.
tell me.
hold me.
have me.
savor me.
love me.

THE TASTE OF SKIN

our tender kiss collapses-
be **careful**, leaks off my lips.
i have a really strong heart;
once she beats for you,
she never really stops.

exhume this love from my body-
it it yours.
it has always been yours.
my body has been waiting for the day
you'd come, the day you'd worship these bones,
the day you'd remind me the meaning of god's
to have and to hold and give me
the gift of loving you.

maybe *the one*
is simply the one within that moment of time.
maybe the one is really
whomever you're bleeding into or within,
whomever's smell is soaked within your skin
after days of being together
and subtle moments of being apart.
maybe **the one** is not of one soul
but is the coming together of two souls
        intentionally.
maybe we have always had it wrong:
maybe the one isn't someone
you're always searching for,
dreaming of matching the patterning
of your soul's desire—
but maybe the one is the frequency
between you and another
as your eyes exchange an inhuman depth,
as your lips intertwine
and your bodies feel like one
interconnected organism.
maybe we've always been right,
maybe the one is an exact moment
where everything feels just right
and your everything is so simply aligned
that all you feel is a yes.
maybe the one is something that happens all across time,
with this one and that one
and maybe even one you never dreamed of.
maybe it's always been all of it,
and could only really be described
to another as this feeling of
this is it.

THE TASTE OF SKIN

i always wondered if this would happen.
i told myself so many times
that my bones were speaking to me.
the earth rose up through me,
showered me in visions of our love,
and yet your name, your melodies
echoed frequencies I used to **wonder**—
how on earth could I be worthy?
if you would even see me?
and yet these dreams told me
there was nothing else for you to know.
that you would wander right into an eternal existence
next to me.

i thought i'd be afraid to love you,
that id be jaded by the reflection
of my shadows within you-
the parts of me that have sabotaged
any opportunity of love i have found before-
but your eyes demand a part of me
to stand within myself and allow you
to reflect the power i have inside me.
it is not a fear i feel bubbling through my veins
but shockingly an excitement
that i may be able to step into all of me
next to you.
i feel **a blue flame** within me
echoes throughout the chambers of my heart-
never had i known the dormancy that laid inside me.
the voice that shatters molds
that beckoned for my throat.
but she is here.
a flame upon a throne
made of my own silken skin.
you haven't scared me off-
you've only pulled me in.

how a name like yours touched my lips.
you were written into my kiss before the stars
and honey, **stars** are my only history
of existence.

you have it,
my heart coiled in your hands-
the slightest compress of your fingertips
and she'll unravel.
i don't caress her walls,
the veins of my soul,
with another's touch often enough
to say the lining of her intimate stature
has been absorbed into another's skin—
for **she**

is too delicate.
and yet there she stands
in the palm of your hands
and i feel ultimately unstable,
knowing a man with such intricate hands
has the ability to rein over me
with his presence.

THE TASTE OF SKIN

you
    were
        always
            there.
                                        it just took me
connecting
        the
                s
                      t
                            a
                                  r
                                        s
                        across
t   i   m   e.
                    allowing the l i n e s   to
  d
   r
    a
     w
          a map
                      toward you.

one that left a sketch of   a
                            l
                            i
                            f
                            e
                            l
                              i
                                n
                                  e
                                    along my path for the

beings who come beyond us

                to walk themselves home.

the story of you and me has been written in the dust of the stars
sprinkled upon us. we chose each other long before
we chose these bodies.

and we knew this walkway would be a love story. a star coded,
soon to be herstory for them. for us. we volunteered to become a new
flame in the new age of what love will be and is becoming.
the intricacies of our weaving are delicate. made for a storybook.
a childhood of stars **born from our bodies.**

i think i've been with you before
the moment our eyes met it's like i knew
your soul as if it were mine,
as if we'd spent a thousand lifetimes falling
in and out of one another.
that's when i knew i was in love.
it was never the actual feeling that brought me closer to you,
but the moment of remembrance i felt
on a celestial level, unexplainably.
a sudden rush down my spine
sent shivers across my entire body,
that was when i knew we could be,
that we could have these memories,
in this life as well as what
we already have in the bank of time.
that's when i knew
as humanly difficult it could be,
it would also be too easy.
that's when i knew that
i've already loved you.
i've already been there with you across time.
maybe in this life i had finally chosen
to open my eternal mind and send myself
into an unknown-
into a place where for once
i'd be caught off guard
and i wouldn't know until i knew,
some force beyond me would drive
an existence of release into a remembrance
of something i believe i've never felt yet,
something i think i've not yet seen,
or asked my soul to be.
something of a friendship
or a presence
or a falling in and out of something
that is simply just me experiencing
heaven's template.

FREYA RAY

i could listen to your voice
for the rest of my life and
it would be the greatest gift
the gods could gift me.

      | a love letter.

to the reader

        firstly, thank you from the absolute bottom of my heart.
thank you for listening. thank you for resonating. thank you even
more for holding the space and heart for poetry in this day and
age. for welcoming the most authentic parts of love into your body
and experience, for being love, for choosing love again and again.

you are love.

in the truest most vulnerable way. this book has become a
mountian for me. i wrote all this poetry along the span of over 5
years. some books truly are meant to be shared in their own
timing and not ours. maybe this message found you for a reason.
if you are someone who has supported the becoming of my soul and
this piece among the many to come of artwork, i value your time
eternally.

thank you
thank you
thank you.

freya ray

about the author

    freya is an author devoted to exploring the symbolic and psychological architecture of the human experience. her work bridges intellect and intuition, weaving together archetypal wisdom spiritual philosophy, and lived inquiry into language that is both grounded and expansive.

through poetry, narrative, and contemplative study, she examines identity, power, longing, and transformation as essential waves within the human experience. rather than offering escape, her writing invites integration- a return to inner authority, critical thought, and embodied self awareness. her work encourages readers to engage deeply with themselves and the unseen patterns shaping their lives. reminding them that their self knowledge is their own blueprint to the living presence of their dreams.

where to find more of freya

instagram | freyarayy
website | www.freyaannerayy.com

Made in the USA
Coppell, TX
10 March 2026

73141002R10108